Little Cooks - a book inspired by the children of
Little Havens Children's Hospice.

Published in the United Kingdom by
Little Havens Children's Hospice in 2007.

Little Cooks

A cook book inspired by the children of
Little Havens Children's Hospice

Photography by Jean Dawkins

Printed September 2007
Editor and Project Manager: Hermoyone Dukes
Photography: Jean Dawkins
Art Direction and Design: SHG Creative

Little Havens Registered Office:
Stuart House
47 Second Avenue
Westcliff on Sea
Essex SS0 8HX

Registered Charity Number: 1022119
Registered Company Name: Havens Hospices
Registered Company No: 2805007

ISBN 978-0-9557345-0-2

www.littlehavens.org.uk

contents

Introduction

"Hannah loved the fairy wonderland for her cakes"
"Lili loves her puddings"
"The mess in the kitchen was well worth it"
"Yum, Yum"
"We are so proud of what we have achieved"

introduction

Welcome to Little Cooks, a book that has evolved from an idea and the inspiration of the children at Little Havens Children's Hospice. Whether you're looking for a new recipe or a new take on an old favourite, we wanted to open up the culinary wonders from the Little Havens kitchens for all to enjoy.

We also have input from the experts of the cooking world showing us how it's done in our Celebrity Treats section, their recipes are sure to get you back into the kitchen!

Our recipes are a mixture of child friendly favourites and some for the more discerning palette.

We couldn't be any more proud of this book if we tried, and we hope you have half as much fun flicking through our recipes and cooking up a treat or two as we did.

We would like to say a huge thank you for buying this book. Thanks to our generous sponsors and helpful retailers, all profits from the book will be going straight back to the hospice. So you see you really are helping to make a difference for the children and families we have the privilege to care for here at Little Havens. If you would like to find out more about the work we do at Little Havens and other ways in which you can get involved visit us at www.littlehavens.org.uk.

Children's and Family Favourites

LITTLE COOKS WARNING: this dish contains nuts

Creamy Chicken & Vegetable Curry

A great way to introduce little mouths to the flavours of the world with this Indian delight.
Serves 8 – 10 people, a real feast.

What do I need?

3 lbs diced chicken

3 large onions, peeled & cut into large dice

5 cloves of garlic, peeled & finely chopped

2" piece of root ginger, peeled & finely chopped

1 small butternut squash, peeled & cubed

1 sweet potato, peeled & cubed

2 carrots, peeled & cut into chunks

1 tbsp mango chutney

1 dtsp garam masala

2 dtsp madras curry powder

1 dtsp ground coriander

1 dtsp ground cumin

6 tsp ground turmeric

6 cardamom pods

1 cinnamon stick

2 tins coconut milk

2tbsp sunflower oil

Fresh coriander & toasted flaked almonds to garnish

Step by step

- Heat oven to gas mark 6, or 200°C. Mix together all of the ground spices and set to one side. Place cubed vegetables, 1 onion, 1 tsp of garlic & ginger combined, 1 tbsp of mixed ground spices, 2 cardamom pods & small piece of cinnamon into a baking tray. Coat evenly and put into oven for approximately 10-15 minutes. Meanwhile heat remaining oil in a large saucepan or wok adding the rest of the onions, garlic and ginger. Stir over a medium heat for 1-2 minutes.

- Add the chicken. Keep stirring to avoid the meat sticking to pan, for 3-4 minutes. Add remaining ground spices, cardamom & cinnamon, continue stirring for a further 3-4 minutes to cook out the spices. Add coconut milk and cook gently for approx 20 minutes. Add vegetable mix and mango chutney, stir well and season to taste – continue to cook until vegetables are soft.

- Serve with basmati rice and garnish with fresh chopped coriander and sprinkle with toasted almonds.

Shepherd's Pie

Another old classic. Annie wondered where the sheep were?
Serves 3 – 4 people

What do I need?

2 lbs potatoes peeled and cut into chunks
1 lb minced lamb
1 medium onion, diced
1 large carrot, peeled and diced
2 sticks of celery, washed and diced

1 bay leaf
¾pt lamb stock
Seasoning
Sunflower oil
Piping bag with a star nozzle

Step by step

- Heat the oven to gas mark 6 or 200°C. Place the potatoes into a saucepan of lightly salted water, bring to the boil and allow to simmer until the potatoes are soft. Drain and set aside ready to make the mash.

- Whilst the potatoes are cooling put a small amount of oil into a saucepan, heat gently, add the onion, carrot, celery and bay leaf. Cook on a medium heat for 3 – 4 minutes stirring. Add minced lamb and continue stirring until meat has browned.

- **Little Cooks tip:** if a lot of fat has come out of meat, you can drain some off at this stage.

- Add the lamb stock, bringing back to the boil, then cook gently for 30-45 minutes. Season to taste.

- Back to the potatoes, mash using warm milk and butter, spoon into a piping bag with a star nozzle. Put the minced lamb mixture into a dish suitable for oven to table. Pipe the mash diagonally across the top of the mixture until dish is covered. Place into the oven for 10-15 minutes until top has become golden.

You can add pretty much anything to the cake mixture; a handful of chocolate chips, sultanas, cocoa powder or even lemon zest.

Fairy Sprinkle Cakes

These cakes are great for the kids to make, especially stirring the mixture and icing them after! Be careful the little ones don't get too close to the oven and make sure they wait until the cakes have cooled down before icing and eating.

Makes 18 cakes

What do I need?

For the Fairy Cakes
225g unsalted butter
225g sifted self-raising flour
225g caster sugar
2 free-range or organic eggs
Few drops of vanilla extract
18 paper cake cases

For the icing
150g sifted icing sugar
Cold water
Food colouring
Sprinkles (Hundreds and Thousands, Smarties, chocolate buttons, jellies)
Muffin tins

Step by step

- Preheat the oven to 190°C/370°F/gas mark 5. Line the muffin tins with 18 paper cake cases.
- Beat together the unsalted butter and caster sugar in a large bowl with a wooden spoon or an electric whisk until light and fluffy.
- Beat the eggs in a jug with the vanilla extract, then beat into the butter and sugar mixture.
- Fold in the sifted flour and then spoon a little mixture into the cake cases. Put the muffin tins into the oven for 12-15 minutes until cooked. Remove cakes from tins and place on a cool rack.
- To make the icing, sift the icing sugar into the bowl and add a few drops of water, stirring constantly till you achieve a dropping consistency. Add a few drops of food colouring and spoon over the cooled cakes.
- Add sprinkles!

Italian Pasta

All pasta is Italian, but with the green pesto, white mozzarella and red sun-dried tomatoes it represents the colours of the Italian flag. This is a great dish when you are strapped for time.

Serves 4
Cooking time 10 minutes

What do I need?

400g linguine or spaghetti
110g pine nuts
250g sun-dried tomatoes in oil
125g mozzarella pearls

8 tbsp green pesto
Salt and pepper
Parsley (optional)

Step by step

- Cook the linguine according to the packet. Meanwhile, lightly toast the pine nuts in a dry pan and put to one side.
- Drain the sun-dried tomatoes and slice in half. Do the same with the mozzarella pearls if they are a bit big.
- Check the linguine a minute before it is ready. The pasta needs to be "al dente" for this dish.
- Drain and put back in the saucepan. Stir in the pesto, and then add the mozzarella, tomatoes, pine nuts and seasoning.
- Garnish with some chopped flat-leaf parsley and serve with warm ciabatta or another Italian bread.

LITTLE COOKS WARNING: this dish contains nuts

Yum Yum Rice Pudding

John certainly had fun making his favourite dessert.
A simple and easy to prepare dish packed with extra yumminess.

Serves 4

What do I need?

2 oz round grain rice
1pt full cream milk
1 oz sugar
¼ pt cream

Step by step

- Rinse the rice until the water runs almost clear.
- Pour full cream milk into a saucepan, stir in the rinsed rice and add the sugar.
- Stir well, bringing to the boil, continue to stir occasionally then simmer for approximately 1 hour until the rice is soft and the mix starts to thicken slightly.
- Add the cream and sprinkle with nutmeg.
- **Little Cooks tip:** serve with strawberry jam for extra Yum Yum.

Profiteroles & Chocolate Sauce

A deliciously messy treat for the whole family! John and Bridie certainly had fun.
This mouth-watering recipe makes 8 – 10 buns

What do I need?

5 fl oz cold water
2 oz butter
For the yummy chocolate sauce
11oz chocolate, melted
¼ pt double cream

For the choux pastry
2½ oz strong plain flour
2 eggs, beaten well
pinch of sugar
For the filling (optional)
1 tsp icing sugar
⅕ pt double cream, whipped

Step by step

→ Heat oven to gas mark 6 or 200°C. Place the 5fl oz of water into a saucepan along with the butter and sugar and bring to the boil. Stir until the butter has melted and remove from the heat. Add all of the flour (2 ½ oz) and stir quickly, return the pan to the heat and stir the mixture. **Little Cooks tip:** stir until the mixture leaves the sides of the pan clean. Remove from heat and allow to cool slightly.

→ Beat the eggs and gradually add to the cooled mixture – a little at a time – beating well between each addition. Place a dessert teaspoon of mixture onto a greased and lined baking tray - remember to leave space for them to rise. You should have enough mixture for between 8 – 10 buns. Place in the pre-warmed oven on the top shelf for approximately 10-15 minutes.

→ For the chocolate sauce break up the chocolate and allow to melt in a bowl over a pan of simmering water – don't let the bowl touch the water! Heat until the chocolate has melted, remove from the heat and add the ¼pt double cream, stir well.

→ Whip together the cream and icing sugar until it forms soft peaks. Make sure you don't over whip it. When the buns have cooled, slit the top and fill with the cream using a spoon or piping bag.

→ Now for the best bit, arrange the buns on a serving dish and pour over the hot chocolate sauce.

Baked Banana with Buttons

This great alternative BBQ dish is one not to be missed.
Serves 4

What do I need?
4 bananas
Packet of chocolate buttons

Step by step
- Make a lengthways split in the bananas - you don't need to peel them! Place the chocolate buttons inside the bananas.
- Wrap in foil and place on the BBQ for 10 minutes.
- Unwrap foil and enjoy.
- **Little Cooks tip:** eat with a spoon to scoop out the delicious mixture.

Fruity Jellies

Great for a picnic treat. Another quickie for mums on the run!
Serves 6-8

What do I need?
Packet of jelly – flavour of your choice
Fresh raspberries

Step by step
- Place some fresh raspberries at the bottom of a small glass dessert bowl.
- Then make up your jelly as per the packet instructions and pour over your raspberries.
- Pop into the fridge to chill.

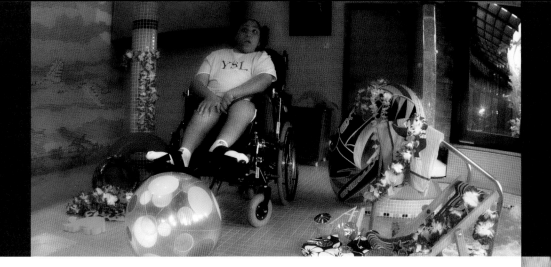

Banana Cocktail

A great way to add a touch of summer magic all year round, and it's full of protein! It certainly chilled Hussan out.

This scrumptious drink serves 1

What do I need?

1 small banana
2 oz thick Greek-style natural yoghurt
1 egg
1 – 2 tbsp light brown sugar or clear honey
Ice

Step by step

▣ Whizz the banana, yoghurt, egg and sugar in a blender with one or two cubes of ice for about two minutes.

▣ Pour into a tall glass and finish with a sprig of mint and if you're feeling really tropical, a colourful umbrella!

▣ Simple, quick and tasty.

LITTLE COOKS WARNING:
this dish contains nuts

Little Cooks Christmas Cake

Serves 10-12

What do I need?

1lb 8oz mixed fruit – to include mixed peel
4oz glace cherries
2 tbsp brandy, sherry or rum
4 eggs
8oz margarine
8oz soft brown sugar

8oz plain white flour
1 tbsp mixed spice
4oz ground almonds
8" round baking tin (or you could use a 7" square tin)
Greaseproof baking paper

Step by step

- Preheat oven to 150°C or gas mark 2.
- Put the mixed fruit and quartered cherries in a bowl, pour over the brandy (or whatever you have chosen) and leave to marinate overnight. Line your baking tin with greaseproof paper. Cream the butter and sugar into a large bowl until light and fluffy. Beat the eggs in a bowl.
- Mix flour and spice in a separate bowl and add soaked fruit and ground almonds. Mix well.
- Add a spoonful of egg to butter mixture, mix well followed by a spoonful of flour mixture. Repeat until all mixture has been added, making sure you mix well at each addition.
- Pour mixture into tin. Wrap a double thickness of newspaper and tie with string. The paper should stand at least 2 inches above the tin.
- Bake for 3-4 hours until firm (use knife test) and cake stops 'singing'. Allow to cool - remove and place on a cooling tray. When cool, store wrapped in greaseproof paper and foil in an airtight container.
- Pour brandy over top once a month (optional). The cake will keep for a year.

Pietastic Banoffi Pie

"Lili loves her puddings" - *Sarah de Cristofano, Lili's Mum.*

Serves 6

What do I need?

8 inch loose bottomed tin
12oz digestive biscuits, crushed
6oz melted butter
1 tin of condensed milk
4 bananas

½ pint whipped double cream
Lemon juice
Grated chocolate
Greaseproof paper

Step by step

→ In a large mixing bowl mix together your crushed biscuits and melted butter. Line your loose bottom tin with greaseproof paper and press your biscuit and butter mixture into the bottom of the tin. Once done, pop into the fridge to set.

→ Place your can of **UNOPENED** condensed milk into a saucepan and cover with water. Bring to the boil. Top up with water regularly for about 2 hours. **REMEMBER** - don't let it boil dry. Remove saucepan from the heat. **Little Cooks tip:** run under water to cool down.

→ Slice your bananas and sprinkle them with lemon juice -- this stops them from going brown. Once cool, open your tin of condensed milk and spread over your biscuit base. Arrange your sliced bananas on top and add your whipped cream. Sprinkle on your grated chocolate and pop in the fridge until you're ready to tuck in.

Celebrity
Treats

Pancake Lasagne

Serves 6-8

What do I need?

Pancakes
2 eggs, size medium
300ml milk
30ml sunflower oil
130g plain flour
Meatballs
100ml olive oil
500g pork mince
4 spring onions, finely chopped
2 garlic cloves, finely chopped
2 large shallots, finely chopped
2 long red chillies, deseeded and finely chopped
1 teaspoon dried oregano, finely chopped
2 tablespoons finely chopped fresh parsley
1 teaspoon finely chopped fresh basil

2 egg yolks
100g fine breadcrumbs
For the sauce
1 tablespoon extra virgin olive oil
I finely chopped onion
1 clove garlic – finely chopped
1 large jar passatta
Béchamel
150ml milk
25g unsalted butter
25g flour
salt and ground black pepper
To assemble
Egg wash
Grated Parmesan

Step by step

➨ **For the pancakes** mix the egg, milk and half of the oil in a jug. Sift the flour into a bowl and gradually beat in the egg mixture to make a smooth batter. Heat 17.5cm (7in) frying pan and wipe some of the oil all over. Pour 1/8 of the batter into the pan, swirling around to spread the batter. Cook for 1-2 minutes until the batter is set and golden on the base. Flip over and cook for a further 1-2 minutes until golden on the base.

➨ **For the meatballs** mix the meat with the spring onions, garlic, shallots, chilli and herbs. Season and then add the egg yolks and half of the breadcrumbs. Roll into small balls and then roll in the remaining breadcrumbs until they are completely coated. Pan fry in the olive oil for about 3- 4 minutes until golden.

➨ **For the sauce** heat the oil in a frying pan, add the onion and the garlic and cook for 3 minutes until soft but not brown. Add the jar of passata and simmer for 10 minutes then add the meat balls and cook for a further 10 minutes.

➨ **For the Béchamel** melt the butter in a small pan and add the flour, stir continuously and cook for about a minute. Add the milk, mixing a bit at a time, stirring (or whisking) all the time to ensure there are no lumps. Continue adding until you have made a smooth white sauce.

➨ Pre-heat oven to 190°C. In a medium baking tray spread some of the béchamel on the bottom, layer with pancakes and then on top of this layer add a layer of meatballs and sauce. Add some more béchamel and drizzle with egg wash and then sprinkle with Parmesan. Continue in this fashion until you finish with a layer of pancakes. Spread any remaining béchamel, egg wash and tomato sauce over the top, sprinkle with grated Parmesan and bake for 30 minutes before serving.

Aldo Zilli

Ainsley
Harriott

Crunchy Nut Apple Cake Bars

What do I need?

285g soft butter
285g caster sugar
285g self-raising flour
5 eggs beaten
225g apples diced
50g sultanas

1 lemon (rind & juice)
pinch of mixed spice
pinch of ground cinnamon
50g demerara sugar
50g chopped nuts

Step by step

- Pre-heat oven to 190°C/160°C fan oven gas mark 5.
- Grease a large baking tray approx 33cm x 28cm then line with baking parchment.
- In a large bowl, mix the butter and caster sugar until lightly creamed, then gradually beat in the flour and eggs to a smooth consistency. Gently stir in the apples, sultanas, lemon rind, juice and the spices.
- Pour the mixture into the lined baking tray and spread out evenly, then sprinkle the demerara sugar and chopped nuts over the top. Cook in the oven for 35-40 minutes.
- Remove from the oven, allow to cool then cut into bars for a mouth-watering treat.

Baked Pumpkin Gnocchi with Roasted Garlic

Serves 4

What do I need?

4 tea cups pumpkin puree
1 cup semolina
1 cup grated Parmesan
125g softened butter

6 whole eggs
250g double cream
5 cloves peeled garlic
fresh thyme
seasoning

Step by step

- Peel the pumpkin and roast in the oven with the garlic and thyme, making sure the tray is covered with tin foil.
- Blitz the pumpkin in a robot mixer until smooth.
- Place into a mixing bowl and add all the dry ingredients.
- Whisk up the eggs and cream and add to the mixture.
- Season to taste.
- Place into a lined gastronome tray and cover with tin foil.
- Bake at 180°C for 35 to 40 minutes.
- When cooked allow to cool and then cut out into any shape you want.

To serve Place the gnocchi onto a baking tray and cover with a few slices of Taleggio cheese and glaze under the grill. Serve on a plate with some pickled fennel and petit salad.

Jean-Christophe
Novelli

Dipna Anand

Gajar Ka Halwa

This dessert can be eaten hot or cold and can be served by itself, with ice-cream or frozen yogurt.

Serves 4

What do I need?

600g carrots
175g milk powder
25g pistachios
50g almonds

400g sugar
50g butter or margarine
¼ lit fresh milk

Step by step

- Peel, wash and grate carrots.
- Put the grated carrots and milk into a saucepan and bring to the boil, cook for about 15 minutes, stirring with a wooden spoon.
- At this point the milk should be absorbed. Add the butter or margarine to saucepan and cook the carrots until they are golden brown (this should take approximately 15 minutes).
- Add the sugar to the carrot pudding and stir constantly whilst continuing to cook.
- Once all the water has evaporated, add the milk powder, cook for no more than 1 minute and take the saucepan off the heat.
- Garnish the carrot pudding with ground almonds and pistachios.

LITTLE COOKS WARNING: this dish contains nuts

Roast Meatloaf with Tomatoes, Garlic and Basil

Meatloaf is like roasted hamburgers – and we all know how nice they are!
Make sure you use lean, good-quality beef or the juices that drip on to the tomatoes might be a little fatty.
Serves 6-8

What do I need?

2 red onions, roughly chopped
1 tablespoon coriander seeds
a large pinch of ground cumin
1kg lean beef mince
2 large free-range or organic eggs
2 tablespoons breadcrumbs

sea salt and freshly ground black pepper
6-8 fresh rosemary sticks, about 10cm long
10 ripe red and yellow cherry tomatoes
2 garlic cloves, chopped
olive oil
a small bunch of fresh basil

Step by step

- Preheat the oven to 220°C/425°F/gas 7.
- Whizz the onions, spices and the meat in a food processor until well chopped together. Pulse in the eggs and the breadcrumbs and season generously with salt and pepper. Tip onto a work surface and shape into 6 or 8 balls.
- Strip the leaves off the bottom of the rosemary sticks, leaving the leaves on the tops (reserve the stripped leaves). Cut the ends of the rosemary sticks at an angle and push a stick through each ball of meat, leaving the tufty, leafy bit sticking out.
- Chop the tomatoes in half and squeeze out and discard most of the seeds. Chop a little more and spread out with the garlic and the chopped-up extra rosemary leaves in 1 or 2 small roasting trays. Season and drizzle with just a little olive oil.
- Place a baking rack over each tray of tomatoes and lay the meatloaf balls on top. Put the tray in the oven for 30 minutes or until the meat is cooked and crisp on the outside. Cover the rosemary sticks with foil if they start to look too brown. The tomatoes taste fantastic with all the meaty juices from the meatloaf stirred in.
- Serve one meatloaf per person with some tomatoes and juices from the tray. Sprinkle with fresh basil just before serving.

Jamie
Oliver

This recipe is taken from How to Cook Book Three and Delia's Vegetarian Collection

Delia Smith

Vegetarian Shepherd's Pie with Goats' Cheese Mash

Although I am not a vegetarian, I really love this alternative version to meat, with its diverse combination of dried pulses and fresh vegetables. It's also extremely popular with veggie customers in our restaurant at Norwich City Football Club.
Serves 4

What do I need?

4 oz (110 g) dried black-eyed beans, pre-soaked and drained
3 oz (75 g) green split peas (no need to soak), rinsed
3 oz (75 g) green lentils (no need to soak), rinsed
2 oz (50 g) peeled carrots
2 oz (50 g) peeled swede
2 oz (50 g) peeled celeriac
1 large onion, peeled
1 small green pepper, deseeded
2 oz (50 g) butter, plus a little extra for greasing
8 oz (225 g) tomatoes
1 heaped tablespoon chopped mixed fresh herbs, such as sage, rosemary, thyme and parsley

¼ level teaspoon ground mace
¼ level teaspoon ground cayenne pepper
salt and freshly milled black pepper

For the topping

4 oz (110 g) soft goats' cheese
1 lb 8 oz (700 g) potatoes, peeled
2 oz (50 g) butter
2 tablespoons milk
1 oz (25 g) Pecorino cheese, grated
salt and freshly milled black pepper

Step by step

→ You will need to soak and drain the black-eyed beans. To do this, wash them under cold, running water and discard any broken ones. If it is convenient, soak them overnight in 2 pints (1.2 litres) cold water. If you need them today and haven't got time to do this, simply bring them up to the boil (using the same quantity of water), boil for 10 minutes and leave them to soak for two hours before draining.

→ Now put the drained beans into a saucepan with the split peas and lentils. Add 1¼ pints (725 ml) boiling water and some salt, cover and simmer gently for 50-60 minutes, or until the pulses have absorbed the water and are soft. Then remove them from the heat and mash them just a little with a large fork.

→ Now pre-heat the oven to gas mark 5, 375°F (190°C), and put the potatoes on to steam. Next, roughly chop all the vegetables, pile the whole lot into a food processor and process until chopped small. Next, melt the butter in a large frying pan over a medium heat, add the vegetables and cook gently for 10-15 minutes, stirring now and then until they're softened and tinged gold at the edges.

→ Meanwhile, skin the tomatoes. Place them in a heatproof bowl and pour boiling water on to them. After exactly a minute (or 15-30 seconds, if they are small), remove them (protecting your hands with a cloth if the tomatoes are hot), slip off their skins and slice them.

→ After that, add the vegetables to the pulses mixture, along with the herbs, spices and salt and freshly milled black pepper to taste. Then spoon the mixture into the baking dish and arrange the tomatoes in overlapping slices on the top.

→ As soon as the potatoes are cooked, place them in a bowl, add the butter, milk and goats' cheese, whisk to a smooth purée, season with salt and freshly milled black pepper and spread the potato over the rest of the ingredients in the dish. Finally, sprinkle over the Pecorino and bake the pie on the top shelf of the oven for 20-25 minutes, or until the top is lightly browned. If you want to prepare this in advance, it will need about 40 minutes in the oven.

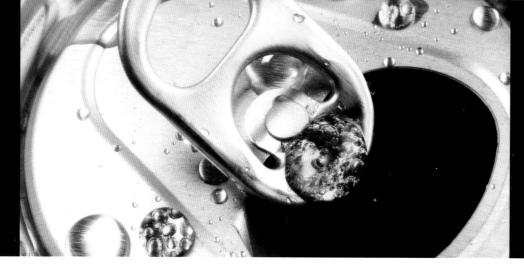

Ham in Coca-Cola

What do I need?

2kg mild-cure gammon
1 onion peeled and cut in half
2 litre-bottle Coke

For the glaze

handful cloves
1 heaped tablespoon black treacle
2 teaspoons English mustard powder
2 tablespoons demerara sugar

Step by step

▣ I find now that mild-cure gammon doesn't need soaking. If you know that you're dealing with a salty piece, then put it in a pan covered with cold water, bring to the boil then tip into a colander in the sink and start from here; otherwise, put the gammon in a pan, skin side down if it fits like that, add the onion then pour over the Coke. Bring to the boil, reduce to a good simmer, put the lid on, though not tightly, and cook for just under 2 1/2 hours. If your joint is larger or smaller work out timing by reckoning on an hour a kilo altogether, remembering that it's going to get a quick blast in the oven later. But do take into account that if the gammon's been in the fridge right up to the moment you cook it, you will have to give a good 15 or so minutes' extra so that the interior is properly cooked. Meanwhile preheat oven to 240°C/gas mark 9.

▣ When the ham's had its time (and ham it is now it's cooked, though it's true Americans call it ham from its uncooked state) take it out of the pan but DO NOT THROW AWAY THE COOKING LIQUID and let cool a little for ease of handling. (Indeed you can let it cool completely then finish off the cooking at some later stage if you want). Then remove skin, leaving a thin layer of fat. Score the fat with a sharp knife to make fairly large diamond shapes, and stud each diamond with a clove. Then carefully spread the treacle over the bark-budded skin taking care not to dislodge the cloves. Then gently pat the mustard and sugar onto the sticky fat. Cook, in a foil lined roasting tin for approximately 10 minutes or till the glaze is burnished and bubbly.

▣ Should you want to do the braising stage in advance and then let the ham cool, clove and glaze it and give it 30-40 minutes, from room temperature, at 180C/gas mark 4, turning up the heat towards the end if you think it needs it.

Nigella Lawson

Gennaro Contaldo

La Gran Lasagne

Serves 6-8

This is not the usual lasagne with a minced meat ragu and cheese sauce which has become so popular all over the world which, when made properly, originates from the Northern region of Emilia Romagna. This is the Neapolitan version of lasagne and would always be made on special occasions such as Christmas or a birthday or christening or any important lunch or dinner. I remember at home, we would make this dish for Christmas lunch and was usually a joint effort between the women in our household. They would get together the day before and my mother would make the fresh pasta sheets, my zia Maria the tomato sauce and my sisters would make the meatballs. Other ingredients would also go into this dish and would include pieces of salami, chicken livers, mushrooms, grilled vegetables and whatever else was around and in season. It was an extremely rich dish and as this usually followed an antipasto (starter) and preceded the main course, it was advisable to take just a little piece. These days, I usually make this as a main course and serve it with perhaps a green salad.

What do I need?

1 x quantity basic fresh pasta 500g
4 x hard-boiled eggs, sliced
4 x packs mozzarella, roughly chopped
200g ricotta
200g Parmesan
flour, for dusting
olive oil, for frying
for the tomato sauce
8 x tablespoons olive oil

2 x medium-sized onion, finely chopped
4 x 400g tins of plum tomatoes
salt & pepper
a couple of handfuls of fresh basil leaves, roughly torn
for the meatballs
250g minced beef
250g minced pork
4 x garlic cloves, finely chopped
3 x tablespoons parsley, finely chopped
1 x egg, beaten

Step by step

- First make the tomato sauce - Heat the olive oil in a large pan, add the onion and sweat until soft. Add the tomatoes, season with salt and pepper and basil, reduce the heat and simmer gently for about 25 minutes. Set aside.

- To make the meatballs - Place all the ingredients in a bowl and mix well together. Shape into small balls, approximately the size of walnuts. Heat some olive oil in a large frying pan. Dust the meatballs with some flour and fry in the hot oil until golden on all sides. Do this in batches, a few at a time depending on the size of your frying pan. Drain on kitchen paper and set aside.

- Preheat the oven to 200°C. Take a large enough ovenproof dish. Line with some of the tomato sauce. Place a layer of pasta sheets, then spoon more tomato sauce over, sprinkle with Parmesan cheese, a few egg slices, a few meat balls, a few knobs of ricotta and pieces of mozzarella. Top with sheets of pasta and repeat with the other ingredients ending up with tomato sauce, meat balls, eggs and cheeses. Cover with aluminium foil and bake for about 30 minutes. Remove the aluminium foil and cook for a further 5 minutes until the cheese has melted nicely over the top.

- Serve immediately.

Wolf Teeth Macaroni

This recipe is baked and served in a large oval dish (or 4 individual dishes). The filling of macaroni cheese and roasted tomato slices is capped around the edges of the dish with big teeth made from thin potato slices cut into the shape of wolf teeth and oven roasted.

Serves 4

What do I need?

Macaroni cheese
225g (8oz) macaroni
40g (1½oz) butter
40g (1½oz) plain flour
560ml (20fl oz) skimmed milk
100g (4oz) cheddar cheese, grated
salt and freshly ground black pepper

Wolves teeth
1 large baking potato
3 tablespoons olive oil
4 large tomatoes, thinly sliced

Step by step

- Preheat the oven to 200°C, 400°F, gas mark 6.
- Cook the macaroni according to the directions on the pack. Drain and leave until required.
- Meanwhile make the cheese sauce by melting the butter in a thick bottomed pan, add the flour and mix together. Cook over a low heat for a couple of minutes, making sure the mix does not colour.
- Slowly add the milk a little at a time, stirring well with a wooden spoon until smooth. Once all the milk has been added, heat until bubbling, take off the heat and stir in the cheese. Season to taste with a little salt and black pepper, cover to keep warm.
- Cut the potato into thin (5mm/¼ inch) slices and cut into triangles for big wolf teeth. Make sure you cut 2 really big teeth (8 if you are making individual dishes) for the fangs in the wolf's mouth. Place in bowl with the oil and then tip onto a baking sheet making sure they are spread out so they brown well.
- Stir the macaroni into the sauce, then pour into a large oval dish (or 4 small oval dishes). Top with tomato slices and roast in the oven with the potato teeth for 15 minutes (10 minutes for individual dishes).
- Watch the teeth do not go too brown as they cook quite quickly. When they are golden remove from the oven and place on kitchen paper to drain off any fat.
- Remove the macaroni cheese from the oven and place the teeth around the edge with the 2 fangs pointing from the top.

What a big red scary mouth - all the better to eat you with!

Kevin Woodford

Staff
Delights

Chocolate Mousse with less calories

A great treat for those on diets or who simply can't resist chocolate! Great if you are in a rush and want something ready to serve in the fridge.

Serves 4

What do I need?
200g plain chocolate
100g quark (curd cheese)
300ml ready to serve 'light' custard
2 tbsp orange juice

Step by step
- Break up the chocolate and place in a bowl suitable for microwave use and cook for 1-2 minutes. Alternatively, melt in a bowl placed over a saucepan over gently simmering water.
- Mix the custard and quark together.
- Stir in the melted chocolate and orange juice.
- Using a piping bag, pipe into shot glasses or small tumblers. Alternatively, pour the mixture into small bowls, little cups or glasses.
- Pop in the fridge to chill for 30 minutes and serve!
- **Little Cooks tip:** grate some white chocolate on top for extra flavour.

Carrot and Coriander Soup

Serves 3-4 hungry mouths

What do I need?
2lb carrots, peeled and cut into slices
1 large onion, peeled and chopped
2 cloves of garlic, peeled and crushed
1 tsp cumin
2 tsp ground coriander
5 cardamom pods, seeds removed and crushed
1 1/2pts vegetable stock
7 oz fresh coriander chopped
1 tbsp sunflower oil
2 oz butter

Step by step
- Heat oil and butter in a large saucepan, then add the slices of carrot, chopped onion and crushed garlic – cook gently for approximately 30 minutes. Stir occasionally, adding the cumin, coriander & cardamom. Stir well for 2 – 3 minutes, adding the vegetable stock, bring to the boil. Add most of the chopped coriander.
- **Little Cooks tip:** keep some coriander by for garnish.
- Allow to simmer for 3 minutes. Remove soup from the heat and blend until smooth, return to heat, season to taste and serve. Delicious with hot crusty bread!

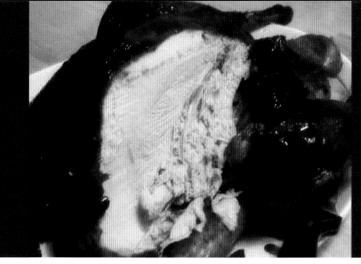

Christmas Spiced Turkey with Cranberry and Chestnut Stuffing

This aromatic turkey, flavoured with traditional festive spices, really brings out the spirit of Christmas. The dark, sticky glaze has just enough sweetness and acidity to cut through the rich white meat.
Serves 6-8

With thanks to James for this mouthwatering recipe

What do I need?

For the Turkey
1 turkey 4.5-5.5 kg
70g butter
1 ½ tbsp honey
1 tbsp port
2 tbsp marmalade
zest of 1 orange
2 tsp ground cinnamon
salt and pepper

For Stuffing
1 ½ celery sticks diced
1 onion diced
3 slices of stale bread
450g sausage meat
2 tbsp sage roughly chopped
1 tbsp thyme roughly chopped
45g roasted chestnuts (or hazelnuts)
50g dried cranberries
2 tbsp port

For Glaze
150 ml turkey stock (or chicken stock)
2 tbsp honey
3 tbsp port
juice of half an orange
1 ½ tbsp marmalade
4 thyme sprigs
4 cloves
1 cinnamon stick

Step by step

- Preheat the oven to 220°C/gas mark 7. Soften the butter and mix in the honey, port, marmalade, orange zest, cinnamon and salt and pepper. Starting at the neck, work your fingers under the skin of the turkey, loosening it and pulling it away from the meat. Using your hands, spread ¾ of the butter mixture under the skin to keep the meat moist, try and cover the breast and as much of the legs as possible. Melt the reserved butter mixture and glaze the turkey. Place in oven for 20 minutes, turn down to 180°C/gas mark 4, cover with foil and cook until done, basting with pan juices every 45 minutes. Plan for 30 minutes per kilo but make sure by skewering the thigh meat. The juices should run clear.

- Whilst the turkey is cooking you can prepare the stuffing. Soak the cranberries in the port for an hour. Add a little olive oil to a pan and sweat the onions and celery until soft. Set aside to cool. Use a food processor to breadcrumb the stale bread. In a large mixing bowl, mix together all the stuffing ingredients, including the port, and shape into 15 balls. Set aside in the fridge until ready to cook. When ready place in an oven, pre-heated to 190°C/gas mark 5, for 25 minutes.

- When the turkey is cooked, set it aside to rest. Transfer the juices to a saucepan and skim off any fat. Using a little stock, deglaze the roasting pan and add to the saucepan with the juices. Add the remaining stock, plus the honey, port, orange juice, marmalade, thyme, cloves and cinnamon to the sauce pan and bring to the boil. Reduce over a high heat until you are left with a sticky, syrupy consistency. Adjust seasonings to taste and strain through a fine sieve.

- Glaze turkey before carving and reserve remaining glaze as a sauce for the table. Serve with traditional festive vegetables and the stuffing.

Steve's Mediterranean Sizzler

Our Head of Care, Steve Lawman cooks up a treat with this Mediterranean medley.

Serves 4

What do I need?

2 tbsp of olive oil
300g chorizo sausage
250g fresh tagliatelle pasta
A generous bunch of flat leaf parsley
A loaf of ciabatta

Step by step

- Chorizo sausage comes in many forms; diced, sliced and whole.
- You can buy it whole then cut it to the size that you fancy.
- Heat the olive oil gently in a frying pan, and then add your sliced/diced chorizo sausage, warming through to release the spicy oils.
- Add the fresh pasta to salted boiling water and cook to taste for 4-5 minutes. Once the pasta and chorizo are cooked add the sausage to the pasta allowing the oil to coat all of the pasta. Top the dish with chopped parsley and warm the ciabatta loaf in the oven before slicing.
- The ciabatta is perfect for mopping up all that spicy chilli and paprika sauce.

CEO's Lasagne

Serves a generous 4

With thanks to Andy Smith, our Chief Executive, for this recipe.

What do I need?

Meat Sauce
1 tablespoon of olive oil
1 large onion, chopped
2-3 cloves of garlic, chopped
6oz/175g button mushrooms, sliced
1 red pepper, chopped
1lb/500g lean steak mince
2 tins of chopped tomatoes
2 tablespoons of tomato puree
fresh or dried herbs (basil, oregano, thyme)
salt and pepper to taste
a dash of Worcester sauce
sheets of lasagne

White Sauce
2oz/50g butter
2 heaped tablespoons of plain flour
1¼ pints of milk
salt and pepper
ground nutmeg
4oz/125g grated cheese

Step by step

- **For the meat sauce** turn on oven, gas mark 5 190°C/375°F. Heat oil in large lidded frying pan or sauce pan. Add onion and garlic, cooking until transparent. Add mince and stir until brown. Add red pepper and mushrooms, and cook and stir for another 2-3 minutes. Add tomato purée and seasoning (herbs and Worcester sauce). Stir. Cover frying pan/saucepan with the lid and cook on a low heat whilst making the white sauce.

- **For the white sauce** make a roux pouring sauce. Melt butter in medium-sized saucepan. Slowly add flour, stirring continuously, to make a roux ball. Gradually add the milk, stirring continuously until sauce thickens. Add salt and pepper and ground nutmeg to taste.

- **Putting it all together.** Spread half the meat sauce over the bottom of a 2 litre oven dish. Cover with sheets of lasagne, just overlapping the edges of the sheets. Spread half the white sauce over the lasagne. Spread the remaining meat sauce over the white sauce. Cover with sheets of lasagne, again just overlapping the edges. Spread the remaining white sauce over the lasagne. Sprinkle the grated cheese over the top. Cook in the oven for 45 minutes.

- Serve with fresh salad, garlic bread (and a good bottle of red wine).

Roasted Vegetable & Pasta in Fresh Tomato Sauce

"A tasty way of getting the kids to eat vegetables" - *Denise Taylor, Little Havens Head Chef.*

Serves 6

What do I need?

2 red onions peeled
2 courgettes
1 aubergine
1 red pepper
1 yellow pepper
1 carrot, peeled & cut into chunks
1 butternut squash
3 garlic cloves, peeled & finely chopped
1 tsp dried oregano

1tbsp olive oil
seasoning
fresh basil
12oz approx pasta of your choice

For the sauce
3 tins of plum tomatoes – chopped
1 tbsp of tomato purée
1 large onion, which you will need to peel and finely chop
1 dtsp of olive oil
seasoning and some fresh basil for garnish

Step by step

- Heat your oven to gas mark 6/200°c. Once you have peeled and chopped your vegetables place them into a large baking tray, cover with olive oil and sprinkle with oregano. Place in oven for approximately 15 – 20 minutes.

- Once cooking away, you can make a start on your tomato sauce. Heat your olive oil in a saucepan, and add your onion and garlic. Cook over a medium heat until the onion is translucent. Add in your tomatoes and purée, stirring well – season to taste and leave to simmer for approximately 20 minutes.

- Not forgetting your pasta, cook as per your packet instructions to "al dente", drain and set aside.

- Once all done, take a large saucepan and mix together your roasted vegetables and pasta, pour over your freshly made tomato sauce, pop on your garnish and serve!

- **Little Cooks top tip:** why not serve with a green salad?

Spicy Parsnip Soup

Serves 3 – 4 hungry mouths

What do I need?

2lb parsnips – peeled and chopped
1 large onion – peeled and diced
2 cloves of garlic – peeled and crushed
2 sticks of celery – washed and chopped
1½ tbsp curry paste (or to taste)

1½ pts vegetable stock
1 tbsp sunflower oil
2 oz butter
seasoning

Step by step

 Heat your oil and butter in a large saucepan.

 Add the chopped parsnips, diced onions, garlic and chopped celery.

 Cook gently for approximately 30 minutes, stirring occasionally.

 Add the curry paste and stir for 2 – 3 minutes.

 Add the 1½pts of vegetable stock and bring to the boil – then simmer for 30 minutes.

 Remove from the heat and blend until smooth.

 Return to the heat and season to taste.

 You are now ready to serve. Easy wasn't it?

Spaghetti Bolognese

"This simple traditional dish is a favourite with the children, even though they do end up wearing it!"
Denise Taylor, Little Havens Head Chef.

Serves 4

What do I need?

1lb minced beef
1 medium sized onion, finely chopped
2 small cloves of garlic, crushed
1 large carrot, grated
1tsp dried oregano

1tbsp tomato purée
1 tin chopped plum tomatoes
1 beef stock cube
seasoning – salt & pepper
olive oil

Step by step

- Place 2tsp of olive oil into a saucepan and heat gently. Add your finely chopped onion and crushed garlic. Keep stirring until your onion is "see through". Add your minced beef and brown. Add your carrots, oregano, tomato purée and tomatoes, stir well and leave it all to simmer for approximately 30 minutes.

- A tip from Denise; if a bit dry add small amount of beef stock, season to taste and leave to simmer for another 20 minutes.

- Whilst you're waiting fill a saucepan with water and lightly salt, bring to the boil. Add your spaghetti and cook as per the packets instructions. Drain and serve on your plate.

- Add your tasty Bolognese. Mmmm.

- **Yummy tip:** serve with garlic bread for extra yumminess.

Chocolate & Orange Cheesecake

Serves 8 chocolate lovers

What do I need?

8" spring clip round tin
4oz butter – melted
8oz choc chip cookies – crushed
200g plain chocolate
200g milk chocolate

1 large orange – zest & juice
400g cream cheese
2oz caster sugar
¾ pt double cream
cocoa for dusting

Step by step

- Add your melted butter to the crushed choc chip biscuits in a bowl and mix together well.
- Press the biscuit mixture into the base of the tin – which needs to be lined with greaseproof paper – and put into the fridge to set.
- Melt the plain and milk chocolate in a bowl placed over a saucepan of hot water. **Little Cooks top tip:** don't allow the water to touch the base of the bowl.
- Add the zest of your orange and 1tbsp of orange juice. Beat the cream cheese and sugar together and whip the double cream until peaking. Gradually fold cream into cheese mixture.
- Stir in the melted chocolate and orange and beat until smooth.
- Pour all over your biscuit base and leave to chill overnight.
- Remove from the tin and dust over with cocoa powder for maximum effect and serve!

Smoked Haddock in Cheese Sauce

It's a family affair for this healthy option dish.
With thanks to Wendy Dodds, our Director of Care, for this family recipe.
Serves 4 hungry mouths

What do I need?

4 smoked haddock fillets
1 pt milk
1 small onion
2 bay leaves
4 cloves
2 oz butter

1 oz plain flour
4 oz mature cheddar
½ tsp mustard
seasoning
fresh chopped parsley

Step by step

- Heat the oven to gas mark 5/190°C.
- Pour the milk into a jug, add the onion, bay leaves and cloves.
- Heat the mixture in a microwave for about 5 minutes.
- Melt the butter in a saucepan adding flour, stir until mixture binds together and leaves the sides of the saucepan clean. Strain the milk onto the flour and butter mixture in small quantities – remember to stir all the time.
- Add mustard and most of the cheese – keep a small amount of cheese to sprinkle over the top of the finished dish. Season to taste.
- Fold the haddock fillets in half and place in an ovenproof dish. Pour sauce over fish and sprinkle on the remaining cheese. Bake in oven for approximately 20 minutes.
- **Little Cooks tip:** garnish with sprigs of fresh parsley and serve with creamy mash and peas.

With thanks to Birgit Duellberg-Webb, care team nurse, for this recipe.

German Apple Cake

Serves 6-8

What do I need?

200g unsalted margarine or butter
4 eggs
200g sugar
lemon juice - you'll need 4 to 5 squirts
150g flour

50g cornflour
½ tsp baking powder
6 or 7 apples depending on size
round cake tin

Step by step

- Heat oven to 175°C.
- Mix the margarine, eggs, sugar and lemon juice together until it reaches a creamy consistency.
- Add the flour, cornflour and baking powder and mix well.
- Grease a round cake tin and fill with half of the cake mixture.
- Peel the apples and cut into quarters.
- Place on top of the cake mixture and then cover with the rest of the mixture.
- Place into pre-heated oven for approximately 45 minutes.
- **Little Cooks tip:** serve warm with vanilla ice cream for extra yum!

Our Grateful
Thanks

thanks...

So many people to thank with so little space! Little Havens would like to take this opportunity to thank those who have worked tirelessly on the preparation and production of Little Cooks.

Firstly, Hermoyone Dukes our Editor and Project Manager for Little Cooks. Her creative vision and relentless drive along with a few sleepless nights made Little Cooks the book it is today.

Special thanks to Jean Dawkins for supplying all of the wonderful photography throughout the book. Jean is a Care Team member at Little Havens and managed to fit in numerous photo shoots around her already busy schedule at the Hospice. Jean the photos are a credit to you.

The incredible children at Little Havens who inspire us on a daily basis, we hope you had lots of fun.

Our families at the Hospice for allowing their children to take part. Our apologies for the messy state we returned them in after the photo shoots – they did enjoy it though!

All the staff who participated in the book, your recipes are delicious and now famous! We also want to thank the rest of the staff behind the scenes who helped look after the children during the photo shoots.

A special mention to Denise, the Head Chef at Little Havens for supplying the Hospice's favourite recipes and for allowing us to make as much mess as we could in the kitchens.

Our grateful thanks to the Celebrity Chefs who have supported Little Cooks - we are so delighted to have you on board.

Big thanks to the guys at SHG Creative for producing yet another wonderful piece of work for the Hospice.

And finally, but by no means least our grateful thanks must go to our Sponsors, without whom Little Cooks wouldn't have been possible. Your generosity and enthusiasm for the project is very much appreciated. A special thanks to IFDS and Hallmark.

Special mention to Louise Warren who came up with the idea in the first place!